Dream Big, Stay Positive, and Believe in Yourself

Dream Big,
Stay Positive,
and Believe in
Yourself

Edited by
Patricia Wayant

Blue Mountain Press™
Boulder, Colorado

We wish to thank Susan Polis Schutz for permission to reprint the following poems that appear in this publication: "A person will get only...," "Dreams can come true...," and "People will tell you...." Copyright © 1983, 1988, 2001 by Stephen Schutz and Susan Polis Schutz. All rights reserved.

Library of Congress Control Number: 2011918551
ISBN: 978-1-59842-640-3

▉ and Blue Mountain Press are registered in U.S. Patent and Trademark Office.
Certain trademarks are used under license.

Printed in China.
Second Printing: 2012

✪ This book is printed on recycled paper.

This book is printed on paper that has been specially produced to be acid free (neutral pH) and contains no groundwood or unbleached pulp. It conforms with the requirements of the American National Standards Institute, Inc., so as to ensure that this book will last and be enjoyed by future generations.

Blue Mountain Arts, Inc.

P.O. Box 4549, Boulder, Colorado 80306

Contents

Dream Big...

There's a field of positive energy surrounding you, just waiting for you to engage it. Go play in this field. Embrace it. Give it a chance to empower you, to love you back. Interact with it. Let the light in and let it light you up. It will help you prepare for anything you have to face in life.

Believe the best of yourself and others. Be open and willing to pamper every important wish in your heart, and especially don't let the big wishes fall through the cracks. Hitch a ride on the wind, a rainbow, or a big, strong eagle in your mind — anything you can. Give yourself every chance you deserve. Think "possible," not "impossible."

Count every single blessing. Let yourself be moved to dance and sing and shout and celebrate, even if it's only on the playground of your heart. Go back to where you've been to understand yourself better, but don't stay in the past. Live each moment. Always smell the roses, but look ahead to where you're going and make good plans.

Swing your arms. Skip your steps. Set yourself free from the don'ts. Enjoy. Believe. Dream.

— Donna Fargo

Reach for the Top

Having a big idea — a dream — will make your life more meaningful. It will give you a focus, a direction. It will give you something to strive for. If your big idea is shot down, simply pick it up, dust it off, and get moving again. Every step toward the fulfillment of your dream will bring immense meaning and satisfaction.

— Kent M. Keith

Set your sights high, the higher the better.
Expect the most wonderful things to happen,
not in the future but right now. Realize that
nothing is too good. Allow absolutely nothing
to hamper you or hold you up in any way.

— Eileen Caddy

Don't put limits on yourself.
So many dreams are waiting to be realized.
Decisions are too important to leave to chance.
Reach for your peak, your goal, your prize.

Realize that it's never too late.
Do ordinary things in an extraordinary way.
Have health and hope and happiness.
Take the time to wish upon a star.

— Collin McCarty

The Dreams in Your Heart
Are Waiting to Come True

Let your goals guide you
　　to the life you are meant to live.
Let your desires remind you
　　to honor the gifts and talents
　　　　you've been blessed with.
Let every challenge strengthen your resolve
　　to achieve all that you were born to do.

Listen to that voice in your heart
　　that tells you to take one more step —
　　　　even when the road is rough.

Live each and every day to its fullest,
　　and let the one-of-a-kind
　　　　person you are shine through.
Share your gifts with the world,
　　and live your dreams.

　　　　　　　　　　　　— Jason Blume

There comes a time in your life when you realize that if you stand still, you will remain at this point forever. You realize that if you fall and stay down, life will pass you by.

Rather than wondering about or questioning the direction your life has taken, accept the fact that there is a path before you now. Shake off the "whys" and "what ifs," and rid yourself of confusion. Whatever was — is in the past. Whatever is — is what's important. The past is a brief reflection. The future is yet to be realized. Today is here. Cast your dreams to the stars.

— Vicki Silvers

Imagine... Here you are, on the high peak of a mountain. You can choose to wing your way toward the clouds, or you can simply walk the usual, ordinary paths that lead to the valley below.

Which choice will you make — the well-worn paths or rising above it all?

Beautiful things await you if you can reach the heights.

— George Sand

Pursue Your Passion

Purpose is knowing
what you want to do
and where you want to go in life.
Passion is letting nothing
stand in the way of getting there.
Passion is the fire inside your spirit,
the force that propels you forward,
and the determination
to make your dreams real.
Passion is the voice inside you
that says "Go for it!"

— Vickie M. Worsham

We do carry an inner light, an inner compass.... It may be small, it may be flickering, but it's actually there. And so what we need to do, I think, is to be still enough to let that light shine and illuminate our inner landscape and our dreams — especially our dreams. And then our dreams will lead us to the right way.

— Alice Walker

Passion is a critical element for anyone who wants to achieve a dream. Why? Because it is the starting point of all achievement. I have never seen anyone anywhere at any time achieve anything of any value without the spark of passionate desire! It provides the energy that makes dreams possible.

— John C. Maxwell

You Have the Power to Make Your Dreams Come True

Get to know yourself —
what you can do
and what you cannot do —
for only you can make your
life happy

Believe that by working
learning and achieving
you can reach your goals
and be successful

Believe in your own creativity
as a means of expressing
your true feelings

Believe in appreciating life
Be sure to have fun every day
and to enjoy
the beauty in the world

Believe in love
Love your friends
your family
yourself
and your life

Believe in your dreams
and your dreams can become
a reality
— Susan Polis Schutz

Put Your Heart into It

Live your life with no regrets.
Reach for a dream
and make it your own.

Be brave enough
to invest a part of your heart
in something real that brings you
great pleasure.

Have a special sense of purpose
and an inner strength
that gives you the confidence
to face each new day
with boldness and courage.

These are just a few
of the beautiful things
that will help you
make your dreams come true.

— Cindy Chuksudoon

Follow Your Intuition

Seek out that particular mental attribute which makes you feel most deeply and vitally alive, along with which comes the inner voice which says, "This is the real me," and when you have found that attitude, follow it.

— William James

People will tell you that you are wrong. It has not and cannot be done! Some will even say you are crazy. But if you feel it is right, pursue your idea, your dream, your creativity. That is what makes new discoveries, beauty, and truth.

— Susan Polis Schutz

Just as you would weigh your decisions carefully, be alert to your instincts and what they are trying to tell you. Spend some time with this innate aspect of yourself. See handling your instincts as an acquired skill — they can give you an edge in many situations, business or otherwise. There are a lot of things we can't see or hear, and our instincts are there to guide us. For example, if you were in the jungle, which would you prefer, a map or a guide? I know I'd feel more comfortable with a guide. A guide has experience and is right there beside you. Your instincts are within you, so use them accordingly.

— Donald J. Trump

Set Goals

It's important to set goals and work hard no matter how many people tell you it's useless and you won't succeed. Without determination, your dreams of a better life won't come true.

— Jackie Joyner-Kersee

I believe in setting goals really high. Then, if you stumble, you still might be very good in the eyes of others. But, if you set them low, once you get there, you're going to be satisfied with what is probably not your best. You're never going to push yourself to achieve even more. That's what dreams are about, aren't they?

— Derek Jeter

We must never be afraid to go too far, for success lies just beyond.

— Marcel Proust

A person will get only what he or she wants
You must choose your goals carefully
Know what you like
and what you do not like
Be critical about what you can do well
and what you cannot do well
Choose a career or lifestyle
that interests you
and work hard to make it a success
Enter a relationship that is worthy of everything
you are physically and mentally
Be honest with people, help them if you can
but don't depend on anyone to make life easy
or happy for you
Only you can do that for yourself
Strive to achieve all that you like
Find happiness in everything you do
Love with your entire being
Make a triumph
of every aspect
of your life

— Susan Polis Schutz

Whatever your goal in life, try to do it to the best of your ability but stay happy. Wherever you set your sights, don't get discouraged, and be proud of every day that you are able to work in that direction. Most of all, along the way, don't forget to stop and smell the roses.

— Chris Evert

It's Never Too Late

Time is relentless.

The days fly by
    faster with each passing year.

We have places to go,
    people to see,
        work to be done,
            errands to run.

"Where does the time go?"
    We ask one another...
        and sigh.

You had dreams once —
    have they faded away?
You had goals and achievements in mind —
    have they fallen by the wayside?
You used to look for love —
    have you given up on matters
        of the heart?
"Seize the day!" you crowed each morning —
    now you settle for seizing a cup
        of coffee instead?

Wake up and smell the coffee...
    or the roses ...
        or the rain.
It doesn't matter what you smell —
    it just matters that you wake up!

What is it you want to BE?
    What is it you want to DO?
        What is it you want to HAVE?

Don't just seize the day —
    seize the rest of your life!

— BJ Gallagher

Stop Procrastinating

When contemplating the pursuit of a dream or the start of a new venture, too many people are hesitant to begin because they can't comprehend the entire journey. If that's where you find yourself right now, don't expect to understand what it takes to get to the top. Just take the next step. There's no shame in starting small; in fact, if you don't start small, you'll probably never start at all.

— John C. Maxwell

Don't be afraid to ask questions. Don't be afraid to ask for help when you need it. I do that every day. Asking for help isn't a sign of weakness; it's a sign of strength. It shows you have the courage to admit when you don't know something and to learn something new.

— Barack Obama

Know the true value of time; snatch, seize, and enjoy every moment of it. No idleness, no delay, no procrastination; never put off till tomorrow what you can do today.

— Earl of Chesterfield

Just Start!

Start by making a small promise to yourself;
continue fulfilling that promise until you have
a sense that you have a little more control over
yourself. Now take the next level of challenge.
Make yourself a promise and keep it until
you have established control at that level.
Now move to the next level; make a promise;
keep it. As you do this, your sense of personal
worth will increase; your sense of self-mastery
will grow, as will your confidence that you
can master the next level.

— Stephen R. Covey

Begin where you are; work where you are;
the hour which you are now wasting, dreaming
of some far off success, may be crowded with
grand possibilities.

— Orison Swett Marden

Whatever you vividly imagine, ardently desire,
sincerely believe, and enthusiastically act upon...
must inevitably come to pass.

— Paul J. Meyer

Someday... You'll See

Someday it will all be worth it. All the hopes, all the dreams. The sacrifices. The courage. All the hard work. All of it will turn out to be abundantly worthwhile.

Someday you'll open the door on a brand-new day and be rewarded with everything working out just the way you wanted it to. So never stop believing in the things you want to come true.

Just start by taking one step in the right direction. Then another. And if you have the faith and the will to continue on, do you know what you'll discover?

How capable you are, how amazing you can be, and how patience and belief can lead to some very meaningful things and some very lasting gifts.

— Chris Gallatin

Stay Positive...

The way you think shapes your world.
A positive attitude can open
the door to limitless possibilities.
When you give yourself
the freedom to dream and imagine,
your world expands.
The impossible becomes possible.
So breathe in peace and hope,
and give your dreams a chance.
Remember, transformation
is not only possible,
it happens every day;
think of butterflies, seeds,
and springtime.

Our world is full of new beginnings.
It is larger than any of us can comprehend.
Take heart, believe in big skies
and wide-open spaces,
and hold on to the promise
of mysteries and magic.
There is space for your dreams to grow.
The future may astonish you.

— Rebecca Brown

Positive thinking is not the destination; it is the journey. An optimistic person will be constantly challenged — by external circumstances as well as inner fears and doubts. Always remember that these tests are like a ladder you must climb. As you move past each rung, your optimism strengthens and your confidence begins to flex newly found muscle that you might never have developed otherwise.

— Montague Edwards

Optimist:

…person who travels on nothing from nowhere to happiness.

— Mark Twain

…someone who isn't sure whether life is a tragedy or a comedy but is tickled silly just to be in the play.

— Robert Brault

Enjoy the Journey

Don't run through life so fast that you forget not only where you've been but also where you're going. Life is not a race, but a journey to be savored each step of the way.

— Nancye Sims

Many of us have road maps we envision for the course we think our lives should take. It's important to get headed in the right direction, but don't get so caught up in the concerns over your destination that you forget to delight in the scenery of each new day. Remember that some of the secret joys of living are not found by rushing from point A to point B, but by inventing some imaginary letters along the way.

— Douglas Pagels

A great attitude does much more than turn on the lights in our worlds; it seems to magically connect us to all sorts of serendipitous opportunities that were somehow absent before the change.

— Earl Nightingale

Let Nothing
Hold You Back

Go forward with your shoulders back, with your head high, and with a smile. With your enthusiastic spirit, perseverance, and integrity of character, put your intelligence, talents, and passion into action.

Never let setbacks excuse you from trying again. It often takes many attempts to be a success.

Never let negative people influence you or direct what you do. Always face forward and see your whole life shining bright for you. Never let go of your character, ideals, or activism for the good of this world.

Never let go of the passions that inspire you, guide you, and always smile on you. These passions will lead you to reach your fullest potential. Hold on to them, and they will keep you honest, caring, kind, and generous with the finest gifts your heart can give.

— Jacqueline Schiff

Forget About Trying to Be Perfect

There are a lot of people who think that what's needed to be successful is always being right, always being careful, always picking the right path.

I think self-knowledge is important and that embraces so many things. It means that when you make a mistake, you realize what it is but you don't beat yourself over the head for it and you don't try to cast blame on somebody else. You don't say, "Life's not fair, I worked hard for this. I deserve this." Finding a sense of balance and a philosophy that can keep you consistent on one level when life is going to be a bumpy and exciting road — that's important!

— Amy Tan

Live Free

Imagine for a moment how you would live your life today if you had nothing to hold you back. In your mind, drop all the fears, insecurities, regrets, anxieties, limitations, worries, and concerns.

Think of the things you would be free to accomplish. Think of the real and lasting value you would be able to create.

Consider all the positive experiences you could craft for yourself and for those around you. Imagine all the steps you could take to make your world a more positive, fulfilling place.

Then stop imagining and start doing. For once you're able to banish the restrictions and limitations from your thoughts, you have greatly reduced their power in your life.

The moment you can visualize being free from the things that hold you back, you have indeed begun to set yourself free. When you sincerely think you are free to act, to move forward, to accomplish, you are.

Travel in your mind to a place where you can live free of past limitations. And know that you are already well on your way there.

— Ralph Marston

Be Willing to Fail

Would you like me to give you a formula for success? It's quite simple, really. Double your rate of failure. You're thinking of failure as the enemy of success, but it isn't at all. You can be discouraged by failure — or you can learn from it. So go ahead and make mistakes. Make all you can. Because remember, that's where you'll find success.

— Thomas J. Watson

I missed more than 9,000 shots in my career. I've lost almost 300 games. Twenty-six times I've been trusted to take the game-winning shot and missed. I've failed over and over and over again in my life, and that is why I succeeded.

— Michael Jordan

I knew that if I failed I wouldn't regret that, but I knew the one thing I might regret is not ever having tried. I knew that that would haunt me every day, and so, when I thought about it that way it was an incredibly easy decision. And, I think that's very good.

— Jeffrey P. Bezos

Don't be discouraged by a failure. It can be a positive experience. Failure is, in a sense, the highway to success, inasmuch as every discovery of what is false leads us to seek earnestly after what is true.

— John Keats

Many of life's failures are people who did not realize how close they were to success when they gave up.

— Thomas Alva Edison

You can't let your failures define you —
you have to let them teach you. You have
to let them show you what to do differently
next time.

— Barack Obama

Find a Way

Every road is sometimes filled with obstacles and defeat, but those are just steppingstones to enable you to go a little further. Stay patient. Your way may be hard right now, but don't give up or let go. Hold on, and travel that road to your dreams.

— Esther Ouellette

Follow where your mind takes you, for once there, anything is possible. And every journey is an inspiration to the soul to make the dream real.

— Author Unknown

I think it's okay, obviously, to acknowledge obstacles and setbacks and problems and issues. But as long as you're dealing with the truth, you're in good shape. I find as long as I acknowledge the truth of something, then that's it. I know what it is and then I can operate. But if I overestimate the downside of something or the challenge of something and I get too obsessed about the difficulty of it, then I don't leave enough room to be open to the upside, the possibility.

— Michael J. Fox

Don't let old mistakes or misfortunes hold you down: learn from them, forgive yourself... or others... and move on. Do not be bothered or discouraged by adversity. Instead, meet it as a challenge. Be empowered by the courage it takes you to overcome obstacles.

— Ashley Rice

When the end of the journey seems impossible to reach, remember that all you need to do is take one more step. Stay focused on your goal and remember… each small step will bring you a little closer.

— Jason Blume

The greatest mistake you can make in life is to be continually fearing you will make one.

— Elbert Hubbard

Always Remember
Who You Are

During troubled times —
  or even during happy,
    carefree times —
remember the depth and core
  of who you are.
Remember your strength
  and inner light.
Remember where you came from
  and where you've been.
Remember that nothing can destroy you.
Life can only make you bigger,
better, and brighter…
if you allow it to do so.
Remember to always
  help light the way for others.
Think of it not as your work
  or even your purpose,
    but as your destiny.
You are empowering and brilliant,
creative and inspiring.
Remember this always
  as you continue being you.

— Jane Almarie Lewis

As Long as You Have Hope,
All Things Are Possible

Hope is found in the way
you look at life.
It's the path you're drawn to follow.
It's in the plans you must arrange,
the goals you want to reach,
the dream that takes
your breath away.

Hope is there when you see
how things can be.
It's the spirit of one who won't give up,
the voice that says it can be done,
and the eagerness to make it happen.

Hope is the belief that anything is possible,
the emblem of one who believes
that dreams can come true,
and the joyous attitude of going forward
to reach every goal.
Most especially, hope brings out
the winner that lives in your heart.

— Barbara J. Hall

Hope sees the invisible, feels the intangible,
and achieves the impossible.

— Charles Caleb Colton

Don't Let Anything Steal Your Joy

Choose to be well in every way. Choose to be happy no matter what. Decide that each day will be good just because you're alive. You have power over your thoughts and feelings. Don't let your circumstances dictate how you feel. Don't let your thoughts and feelings color your situation blue or desperate.

Even if you don't have everything you want, even if you're in pain or in need, you can choose to be joyful no matter what you're experiencing. You are more than your body, your physical presence, and your material possessions. You are spirit. You have your mind, heart, and soul, and there is always something to be thankful for.

Decide that life is good and you are special. Decide to enjoy today. Decide that you will live life to the fullest now, no matter what. Trust that you will change what needs changing, but also decide that you're not going to put off enjoying life just because you don't have everything you want now. Steadfastly refuse to let anything steal your joy. Choose to be happy… and you will be!

— Donna Fargo

Make Each Day
of Your Life...

A Gift...

Greet it with a grateful heart. Imagine your future. Make some new plans. Remember your uniqueness. Reflect on how much you are loved.

A Present to Yourself...

Do something fun, special, magical, and memorable. Appreciate your gifts. Recognize your talents. It's really okay to concentrate on you. Be thankful for what makes you you.

A Time to Celebrate…

The greatest gift you've been given is you. Celebrate yourself… with hope, with joy, with appreciation. Dare to dream. Open your heart and let yourself go as far as your mind will take you. Drop any regrets and negative thoughts that hold you down.

A Day to Be Happy…

Count your blessings; love your life; treasure your family and friends and all that you're thankful for. Above all, soak in the gift of each moment and enjoy it with all your heart.

— Donna Fargo

Believe in Yourself...

Believe in all you want to be. Be happy with who and where you are. You are in the right place, and your heart is leading you to a great tomorrow. When circumstances seem difficult, pull through them. This will make you stronger than you think. The longer you practice the habit of working toward your dreams, the easier the journey will become.

— Ashley Rice

Have faith in yourself. If you do, you will be amazed at what you can accomplish.

— T. L. Nash

Harness the Power
of Self-Esteem

To hold something in esteem means to hold it in favorable regard, to consider it valuable. Self-esteem is to hold yourself in high regard, to think of yourself as a hot property, a uniquely valuable individual, a one-of-a-kind collector's item.

Many people blame their low self-esteem and feelings of inferiority on others. But you cannot have low self-esteem thrust upon you without your permission. You can't be stepped on again and again unless you lie down and let people step all over you.

You always have the choice: pick yourself up off the floor, get up and go forward, or lie there and play dead. If you choose to move ahead, you are emancipated; from that point on, you are 100 percent responsible for your self-image.

To harness the power of self-esteem and make it work for you, begin by acknowledging that you have the free will and free choice to take full responsibility for who you are, how you see yourself, and what direction you're going to point yourself in. There's only one person who can lift your low self-esteem and raise it up to the heights of self-love and self-confidence, and that's you.

— Wally Amos

Don't Ever Lose Sight
of the Wonderful
Person You Are

Life can disappoint you sometimes, and things happen that you didn't expect and don't deserve. But don't ever downplay your abilities. Keep living your life the best way you know how — with persistence, patience, and determination. Let go of the bad things and keep the good.

There is so much ahead waiting for you: chances for new adventures, possibilities you never even dreamed of, and so many people who love you.

Take the time to rediscover yourself. Picture what you want to come into your life. Choose happiness and keep believing in the wonderful person you are.

— Vickie M. Worsham

You have so much to offer,
    so much to give, and
    so much you deserve
    to receive in return.
Don't ever doubt that.

Know yourself and all of your fine
    qualities.
Rejoice in all your marvelous strengths
    of mind and body.
Be glad for the virtues that are yours,
    and pat yourself on the back for all
    your many admirable achievements.

Keep positive.
Concentrate on that which makes you happy,
    and build yourself up.
Stay nimble of heart,
    happy of thought,
    healthy of mind, and
    well in being.

— Janet A. Sullivan-Bradford

When you come to believe
    in all that you are
and all that you can become,
there will be no cause for doubt.
Believe in your heart,
    for it offers hope.
Believe in your mind,
    for it offers direction.
Believe in your soul,
    for it offers strength.
But above all else...
    believe in yourself.

— Leslie Neilson

Write Your Own Life Story

Each day is like a blank page, but it's more than just some story you're writing. It's your life story, and you determine how the story ends. There will be situations you didn't plan on and challenges you didn't bargain for, but with this gift called life comes the potential to make your dreams come true.

Always keep in mind that what you do today will have an impact on tomorrow. Think about how you can take care of yourself. What will you do about your dreams — will you put off getting serious about them or prove to yourself that you mean business?

Love your life. Make the most of each and every day. Be thankful. Learn all you can. Remember: you are the author of your life story, and you can make your dreams come true.

— Donna Fargo

If you think of your life as a story that gradually unfolds, you will embrace the changes and more fully appreciate the moments. You will know how natural it is for new chapters to begin and for the characters and events to surprise you every now and then. You will cherish your heroes and overcome your foes. And you can still have a beautiful story even if it hasn't been great all along. Make the best of everything, and... always enjoy reading the page you're on!

— Douglas Pagels

Today is your greatest opportunity — seize it! Don't look back and wish you had done more yesterday; don't look ahead and get overwhelmed by what may lie there. Do the best you can in this moment with the tools you have at hand. Know that each step you take, no matter how small it may seem now, will, over time, add up to a tremendous journey of discovery on your way to achieving whatever you dream of doing.

— Avery Jakobs

Life is a blank page,
an open highway,
a ticket with your name on it.
Life is a friend and a dream
and a pencil in your hand.
Life is where the day takes you
and what you've got
in your back pocket.

Life is kicking back over coffee,
talking about where
we have been,
walking along on the same road.
Life is a long story
and a song that continues.
Life is all this.
Life is today.
— Ashley Rice

Make Your Own Future

Tomorrow is yours to create.
There's so much potential inside you...
in every dream you hold close
and in each hope that is important to you.
Dance your way to the stars,
dream tomorrow into being,
and celebrate each step along the way.
Expect great things,
and they will be yours someday.

— Linda E. Knight

Be strong about what you believe in. Be firm about who you really are — plus and minus. Know what you will and won't do to get ahead. Know what you can and cannot live with....

You have to take the time to stop and have a conversation with yourself.

— Maria Shriver

I'd like to do everything I can to avoid being an old person who says, "Why didn't I do that? Why didn't I take that chance?"

— Barbra Streisand

Inventory

As I look at my life right now,
It lays in pieces,
Scattered around me on a large wooden floor.
I pick up the pieces one by one,
Check them out,
And take inventory.

I count up the blessings
Against the curses.
I count up the friends
Against the enemies.
I count the possibilities
Against the roadblocks.
And I take stock of my life.

I place all the good pieces of my life
Into a large wooden box.
They fill the box so much I cannot close it.
I start to sweep up the bad pieces,
And as I gather them up,
I am puzzled.
For as much trouble as these pieces caused,
And as much as they weighed on my heart, my soul,
There really wasn't all that much to them.

As I throw them upward
And scatter them to the wind,
I am glad to find
That in my life's inventory,
The pieces of good
Outweighed the bad.

— Ashley Levesque

Have Courage

It takes courage to put one foot in front of another.
Courage to move ahead with life when you aren't
  sure where the road is taking you.

Courage is not shown by taking huge leaps
  and bounds;
Courage is shown in the small steps that we
  take each day...

When we smile as we hurt,
When we move ahead even though we can't see,
When we reach out through our fear,
When we extend our hearts toward the unknown.

Small steps... minute by minute... hour by hour...
  day by day.
Small steps over time lead to larger accomplishments.
Start your day with small steps.
Soon you will see all the future's possibilities lying
  before you.

— Brenda Hager

Only those who will risk going too far
can possibly find out how far one can go.

— T. S. Eliot

Persevere

I do not think there is any other quality so essential to success of any kind as the quality of perseverance. It overcomes almost everything, even nature.

— John Davidson Rockefeller, Sr.

I think it's important to believe in yourself and when you feel like you have the right idea, to stay with it.

— Rosa Parks

If you want to be successful in a particular field of endeavor, I think perseverance is one of the key qualities. It's very important that you find something that you care about, that you have a deep passion for, because you're going to have to devote a lot of your life to it.

— George Lucas

Life is not easy for any of us. But what of that? We must have perseverance and above all confidence in ourselves. We must believe that we are gifted for something and that this thing must be attained.

— Marie Curie

Don't Ever Lose Faith in Yourself

Trust your decisions and feelings
and do what is best for you.
Don't let anyone else's negativity
influence your dreams, values,
   or hopes.
Focus on what you can change
and let go of what you can't.
You know your own worth,
what you've accomplished,
and what you're capable of.
Step boldly and confidently
   into your future
where happiness, success,
and dreams await you.

You have the potential
   for greatness...

never give up.

— Barbara Cage

See Yourself as the Person You've Always Wanted to Be

There may be days
when you get up in the morning
and things aren't the way
you had hoped they would be.
There may be times when people
disappoint you and let you down.
There will be challenges to face
and changes to make in your life,
and it is up to you to
constantly keep yourself headed
in the right direction.
It may not be easy,
but in those times of struggle
you will find a stronger sense
    of who you are,
and you will also see yourself
developing into the person
you have always wanted to be.

— Deanna Beisser

There is nothing to stop you
from reaching out
and touching your star.
Everything you want can be a reality.
All you have to do is truly believe
and feel the energy of it
deep inside your heart —
and it will come to life
before your very eyes.
You are the creator of your destiny;
you have that power within you.
Don't let go of your dreams —
they belong to you alone,
and all of them are available to you.
All you have to do is ask…
then open your heart to receive
all the magnificent gifts
this universe has to offer.

— Lisa Butler

Never Give Up

No matter what you do,
don't ever stop believing in
your most treasured dreams.
The horizon of tomorrow
may hold surprises
that will make things better
than you ever imagined.

So never give up hope,
and don't ever stop working on
the changes you'd like to make
and the goals you would love to achieve.

Just move ahead one day at a time,
and — as the saying goes —
keep your eyes on the prize.

If you keep on doing your best,
the rest will follow.

— Chris Gallatin

If you never dream,
you will never reach the summit.
You will never chart the seas.
You will never soar with eagles.
Your cup will never overflow.
You'll never touch the rainbow.
You'll never scale the mountain.
The world will never find peace.
A great cure will never be found.
You will never touch the stars.

If you never dare to dream,
you will never be all that you can be.
You will never give voice to the poet,
give sight to the artist,
give life to the writer,
or give back to the world all
that it's possible for you to return.
Never stop dreaming.
Never give up.
Always look up,
and the stars will appear.

— Brenda Hager

Make Your Dreams Come True

The path to a dream is paved
    with sacrifices
and lined with determination.
And though it has many stumbling blocks
    along the way
and may go in more than one direction,
    it is marked with faith.
It is traveled by belief and courage,
    persistence and hard work.
It is conquered with a willingness
to face challenges and take chances,
    to fail and try again and again.
But when the path comes to an end,
you will find that there is no greater joy
than making your dream come true.

— Barbara Cage

Let nothing hold you back from exploring your wildest fantasies, wishes, and aspirations. Don't be afraid to follow your dreams wherever they lead you. Open your eyes to their beauty; open your mind to their magic; open your heart to their possibilities.

— Julie Anne Ford

Dare to live the life you have dreamed for yourself. Go forward and make your dreams come true.

— Ralph Waldo Emerson

Acknowledgments

We gratefully acknowledge the permission granted by the following authors, publishers, and authors' representatives to reprint poems or excerpts from their publications.

PrimaDonna Entertainment Corp. for "Don't Let Anything Steal Your Joy," "There's a field of positive energy…," "Make Each Day of Your Life…," and "Each day is like a blank page" by Donna Fargo. Copyright © 2005, 2006, 2010, 2012 by PrimaDonna Entertainment Corp. All rights reserved.

G. P. Putnam's Sons, a division of Penguin Group (USA), Inc., for "Having a big idea…" from ANYWAY: THE PARADOXICAL COMMANDMENTS by Kent M. Keith. Copyright © 2001 by Kent M. Keith. All rights reserved.

Findhorn Press, Scotland, for "Set your sights high…" from OPENING DOORS WITHIN by Eileen Caddy, edited and compiled by David Earl Platts. Copyright © 1986, 2007 by Eileen Caddy. All rights reserved.

Jason Blume for "When the end of the journey…" and "The Dreams in Your Heart Are Waiting to Come True." Copyright © 2005, 2012 by Jason Blume. All rights reserved.

Vickie M. Worsham for "Purpose is knowing what you want…." Copyright © 2012 by Vickie M. Worsham. All rights reserved.

Marianne Schnall for "We do carry an inner light…" by Alice Walker from "Conversations with Alice Walker" (www.feminist.com: December 26, 2006). Copyright © 2006 by Marianne Schnall. All rights reserved.

Thomas Nelson, Inc., Nashville, TN, www.thomasnelson.com, for "Passion is a critical element…" from PUT YOUR DREAM TO THE TEST by John C. Maxwell. Copyright © 2009 by John C. Maxwell. All rights reserved.

Perseus Books Group for "Just as you would weigh your decisions…" from THINK LIKE A CHAMPION by Donald J. Trump. Copyright © 2009 by Donald J. Trump. All rights reserved.

Grand Central Publishing for "It's important to set goals…" from A KIND OF GRACE by Jackie Joyner-Kersee. Copyright © 1997 by Jackie Joyner-Kersee. Reprinted by permission of Grand Central Publishing. All rights reserved. And for "Be strong about what you believe in" from TEN THINGS I WISH I'D KNOWN BEFORE I WENT OUT INTO THE REAL WORLD by Maria Shriver. Copyright © 2000 by Maria Shriver. Reprinted by permission of Grand Central Publishing. All rights reserved.

Crown Publishers, a division of Random House, Inc., for "I believe in setting goals really high" from THE LIFE YOU IMAGINE by Derek Jeter and Jack Curry. Copyright © 2000 by Turn 2, Inc. All rights reserved.

Chris Evert for "Whatever your goal…" from CHRISSIE, MY OWN STORY. Copyright © 1982 by Evert Enterprises, Inc. All rights reserved.

BJ Gallagher for "It's Never Too Late." Copyright © 2012 by BJ Gallagher. All rights reserved.

GiANT Impact, www.giantimpact.com, for "When contemplating the pursuit…" from "Think Big, Start Small" from "Leadership Wired" by John C. Maxwell. Copyright © 2006 by John C. Maxwell. All rights reserved.

Barack Obama for "Don't be afraid to ask questions" and "You can't let your failures…." Copyright © 2009 by Barack Obama. All rights reserved.

Dr. Stephen R. Covey, www.stephencovey.com, for "Start by making a small promise…" from PRINCIPLE-CENTERED LEADERSHIP. Copyright © 1992 by Stephen R. Covey. All rights reserved.

The Leading Edge Publishing Company, www.theleadingedgepublishing.com, for "Whatever you vividly imagine…" by Paul J. Meyer. Copyright © 1997 by Paul J. Meyer. All rights reserved.

Robert Brault, www.robertbrault.com, for "Optimist: someone who isn't…" from "Six Definitions of an Optimist" (*A Robert Brault Reader*: June 28, 2009). Copyright © 2009 by Robert Brault. All rights reserved.

Diana Nightingale, www.earlnightingale.com, for "A great attitude does much more…" from "The Magic Word" audio program by Earl Nightingale. Copyright © 2011 by Earl Nightingale. All rights reserved.

Academy of Achievement, www.achievement.org, for "If you want to be successful…" by George Lucas from "A Life Making Movies," "I knew that if I failed…" by Jeffrey P. Bezos from "Inventing E-Commerce," "There are a lot of people…" by Amy Tan from "A Uniquely Personal Storyteller," and "I think it's important to believe…" by Rosa Parks from "Interview: Rosa Parks." Copyright © 1995, 1996, 1999, 2001 by Academy of Achievement. All rights reserved.